LIFE STORIES

FRANKLIN D. ROOSEVELT

Gillian Gosman

PowerKiDS
press™

New York

Published in 2011 by The Rosen Publishing Group, Inc.
29 East 21st Street, New York, NY 10010

First Edition

Editor: Jennifer Way
Book Design: Ashley Burrell and Erica Clendening

Photo Credits: Cover (main, background), pp. 15, 22 (top) George Skadding/Time & Life Pictures/ Getty Images; pp. 4–5, 6, 11 (bottom), 13 Hulton Archive/Getty Images; pp. 7, 12 Popperfoto/ Getty Images; p. 8 Transcendental Graphics/Getty Images; pp. 9, 16 FPG/Getty Images; p. 10 Topical Press Agency/Getty Images; pp. 11 (top), 14 MPI/Getty Images; p. 17 Fox Photos/Getty Images; pp. 18–19 U.S. Army Signal Corps/Time & Life Pictures/Getty Images; pp. 19 (inset), 22 (bottom) American Stock/Getty Images; pp. 20–21 Altrendo Travel/Getty Images.

Library of Congress Cataloging-in-Publication Data

Gosman, Gillian.
 Franklin D. Roosevelt / by Gillian Gosman. — 1st ed.
     p. cm. — (Life stories)
 Includes index.
 ISBN 978-1-4488-3179-1 (library binding) — ISBN 978-1-4488-3182-1 (pbk.) —
 ISBN 978-1-4488-3183-8 (6-pack)
 1. Roosevelt, Franklin D. (Franklin Delano), 1882-1945—Juvenile literature. 2. Presidents—United States—Biography—Juvenile literature. 3. United States—History—1933-1945—Juvenile literature. I. Title.
 E807.G677 2011
 973.917092—dc22
 [B]
                            2010038439

Manufactured in the United States of America
CPSIA Compliance Information: Batch #WW11PK: For Further Information contact Rosen Publishing, New York, New York at 1-800-237-9932

CONTENTS

MEET FRANKLIN D. ROOSEVELT

In 1933, President Franklin D. Roosevelt gave his first fireside chat. This was a speech on the radio about the president's plans for the country. Every president since Roosevelt has given speeches like this.

Roosevelt was a man who wanted to try new ideas. He led America through the **Great Depression** and **World War II**. These were some of the hardest times the country had ever faced.

Roosevelt is the only U.S. president to serve more than two terms. He was reelected in 1936, 1940, and 1944.

Young Franklin

Franklin Delano Roosevelt was born in Hyde Park, New York, on January 30, 1882. His family was rich and well-known. Roosevelt went to Harvard University and then Columbia Law School.

Here is Roosevelt with his mother (left), his daughter Anna (second from right), and two of his grandchildren.

Eleanor and Franklin were distant cousins.
Eleanor's uncle was President Theodore Roosevelt.

Roosevelt was a very good student. He passed the test to become a lawyer before he finished law school!

In 1905, he married Anna Eleanor Roosevelt. The Roosevelts would have six children, five of whom would live to be adults.

Life During the Great Depression

Roosevelt became president during the Great Depression. On October 29, 1929, the **stock market** crashed. This caused many people and businesses to lose all of their money.

During the Great Depression, soup kitchens fed many people.

The day of the stock market crash became known as Black Tuesday because it was an unhappy day.

The Great Depression was the worst **economic** time in American history. As president, Roosevelt needed to help Americans and the economy.

The Young Politician

In 1910, Roosevelt was **elected** to the New York State Senate. In 1920, he ran as the Democratic **candidate** for vice president of the United States. He lost the election and left politics for a few years.

Here is Roosevelt with James Cox in 1920 when they were running for president and vice president.

This is a poster from when Cox and Roosevelt were running as Democratic candidates for president and vice president.

In 1921, Roosevelt caught polio. This illness left him **paralyzed** from the waist down. This meant that he would never walk again. In 1928 and again in 1930, Roosevelt was elected governor of New York.

Roosevelt used a wheelchair because polio had left him unable to walk.

PRESIDENT ROOSEVELT

In 1932, the United States was in the middle of the Great Depression. President Herbert Hoover, a Republican, was against starting programs to help people who were hurt by the Depression.

Here is Roosevelt during his 1932 run for president.

Herbert Hoover lost the 1932 presidential election to Roosevelt.

Roosevelt ran as the Democratic presidential candidate in 1932. He promised to begin programs to help the country recover from the Depression. Roosevelt won the election.

THE FIRST HUNDRED DAYS

During his first 100 days as president, Roosevelt started many programs. These programs were known as the New Deal because they promised Americans a fresh start at life.

Roosevelt's New Deal programs were meant to help people who were hurt by the Great Depression.

Roosevelt gave speeches called fireside chats. These speeches played on radio stations across the country.

Roosevelt started programs that gave food, housing, and work to the people who needed it. He also passed laws that helped control the country's banking system.

15

THE NEW DEAL

The New Deal is best known for its many projects. The Tennessee Valley Authority built dams across the South. This helped stop flooding and brought electricity to many places.

The Civilian Conservation Corps was a New Deal program that gave people jobs in national parks and forests.

Here is Roosevelt speaking before a crowd in New York City in 1940.

The Federal Writers' Project sent writers around the country to record stories and music from people. The Social Security Act gave money to people who were out of work and to older Americans.

THE PRESIDENT AT WAR

World War II began in Europe in 1939. On December 7, 1941, the Japanese navy attacked the U.S. **naval base** at Pearl Harbor, Hawaii. This attack drew the United States into the war.

Here is Roosevelt with Winston Churchill (left) of Great Britain and Josef Stalin (right) of the Soviet Union.

The United States and the other **Allied nations** won the war. The war ended on September 2, 1945. Roosevelt would not live to see this day, though.

The attack on Pearl Harbor drew the United States into World War II.

19

An Early End

By 1944, Roosevelt was in bad health. He died on April 12, 1945.
    Roosevelt led the country through the Great Depression and World War II. Some of

This is the Roosevelt memorial in Washington, D.C. Roosevelt is shown with his dog, Fala.

the programs he started, such as Social Security, are still going today. He is widely thought of as one of America's greatest presidents.

TIMELINE

January 30, 1882

Roosevelt is born in Hyde Park, New York.

1921

Roosevelt gets polio.

1933–1945

Roosevelt is president. He is elected to four terms.

April 12, 1945

Roosevelt dies.

December 7, 1941

Japan attacks Pearl Harbor. The United States enters World War II, which lasts until 1945.

1933

Roosevelt begins his New Deal plans.

Glossary

Allied nations (uh-LYD NAY-shunz) The countries that fought against Germany, Japan, and Italy in World War II. The Allies were Great Britain, China, France, the Soviet Union, and the United States.

candidate (KAN-dih-dayt) A person who runs in an election.

economic (eh-kuh-NAH-mik) Having to do with the production and supply and demands of goods and services.

elected (ee-LEK-tid) Picked for an office by voters.

Great Depression (GRAYT dih-PREH-shun) A period of American history during the late 1920s and early 1930s. Banks and businesses lost money and there were few jobs.

naval base (NAY-vul BAYS) A place where a country's navy houses its sailors and its ships.

paralyzed (PER-uh-lyzd) To have lost feeling or movement.

stock market (STOK MAR-ket) A market for buying shares, or part ownership, in companies.

World War II (WURLD WOR TOO) A war fought by the United States, Great Britain, France, China, and the Soviet Union against Germany, Japan, and Italy from 1939 to 1945.

Index

Web Sites

Due to the changing nature of Internet links, PowerKids Press has developed an online list of Web sites related to the subject of this book. This site is updated regularly. Please use this link to access the list:
www.powerkidslinks.com/life/fdr/